Dis

Meditations for 40 Days of Lent

Carol Mead

Forward Movement

Morehouse Publishing

Copyright © 2012 Forward Movement

All rights reserved.

Cover design: Albonetti Design

Printed in the United States of America

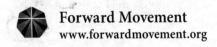

Disciples on the Way

Meditations for 40 Days of Lent

Carol Mead

Foreword

Disciples on the Way is a guidebook for a journey through Lent that reflects on the season through passages from *The Book of Common Prayer*. Often called simply the "Prayer Book," this collection of prayers, hymns, biblical passages, and other texts frames the public worship of The Episcopal Church. In this Lenten booklet, each selection from *The Book of Common Prayer* provides a starting place to consider what being disciples of Christ in our everyday lives looks like.

The Book of Common Prayer can be found in any Episcopal Church in your community. It can also be read or downloaded online for free at www.episcopalchurch.org/page/book-common-prayer or purchased from Church Publishing at www.churchpublishing.org or by calling 800.409.5346.

Ash Wednesday

Almighty and everlasting God...
Create and make in us new and contrite hearts,
that we, worthily lamenting our sins and
acknowledging our wretchedness,
may obtain of you, the God of all mercy,
perfect remission and forgiveness.

— Collect for Ash Wednesday, p. 264

In the western Christian tradition, Lent begins on Ash Wednesday and culminates in our celebration of the resurrection on Easter Sunday. In modern times, Lent has become widely known as a time when we "give something up." But to see Lent only as a time of self-deprivation diminishes the power of the season. Truly, Lent is a time to practice discipline—not for discipline's sake, but to become more aware of choices that separate us from God.

The words "discipline" and "disciple" both originate from Latin root words that speak of pupils and teaching. In Jesus' earthly life, he taught his followers that discipleship required commitment, sacrifice, and a determination to turn the world toward God. Jesus' message to us is much the same, so we are called to spend this season of Lent learning how to serve Christ intentionally, faithfully, and joyfully.

We become disciples of Jesus, in part, to learn how the Spirit of God works in human circumstances. Because the Christian faith celebrates the incarnation of divine Spirit in human flesh, we continually explore the interrelationship of the spiritual and physical dimensions of human life. Observing Lent may reveal to us ways of worship, study, prayer, and action that make us more acutely aware that God is present in us and with us. Such practices help us to blend the spiritual with the physical, the unseen with the seen, the transcendent with the mundane.

In the Collect for Ash Wednesday, we ask God to "Create and make in us new and contrite hearts." That fine old-fashioned word, "contrite," comes from another Latin word meaning to grind or bruise. A valuable lesson of Lent comes when we realize that we cannot truly be disciples of Jesus

Christ and remain comfortable with the way the world is. If our faith is to grow into something meaningful, something more than a pious hobby, we will have to endure some discomfort. We don't need to beat ourselves up, but the injustice of the world should grind and bruise us enough that we are willing to do something to change it.

After all, a contrite heart in itself does nothing to usher in the kingdom of God. In fact, people who call themselves "spiritual but not religious" may resist the Christian tradition partly because they perceive that we are proud of our contrite hearts. And people within that Christian tradition experience less depth and joy when they think contrition is the primary goal. To be productive, contrition has to make us aware of injustice and poverty—material and spiritual—and move us to do something about them.

And so our journey through Lent begins on Ash Wednesday with a renewed invitation to move toward discipleship and a life that truly embodies and celebrates our knowledge of the risen Christ. Because we are human—made for union with God and our fellow human beings—in this Lenten season we turn our hearts and minds to contrition to find wholeness in God and then pass that healing and forgiveness on to others. But we do well to remember that productive contrition will almost certainly involve some bruising and grinding.

Lord, guard us from becoming too comfortable with the injustice of this world.

Thursday after Ash Wednesday

Hear what our Lord Jesus Christ saith:
Thou shalt love the Lord thy God with all thy heart,
and with all thy soul, and with all thy mind.
This is the first and great commandment.
And the second is like unto it:
Thou shalt love thy neighbor as thyself.
On these two commandments
hang all the Law and the Prophets.

— The Holy Eucharist: Rite One, p. 324

One day in grade school, I was with a fellow student who needed to call home. Unable to remember the number, he opened the phone book and started scanning every name from A to Z. He didn't know the names were listed in alphabetical order. His search would have been considerably shorter if he had known the system behind the book.

In sorting through the noise of human life, it helps to identify an organizing principle, a unifying framework behind the details. For me, as a Christian, the belief that God is love unifies my pursuit of all truth about God.

Early in the Rite One Eucharistic service of The Episcopal Church, we hear the commandments to love God and our neighbor followed by the reminder, "On these two commandments hang all the Law and the Prophets." Those words identify love as the unifying principle behind all that we do.

Seeing love as the bottom line helps in all of Christian practice. We can navigate conflicts and contradictions in Scripture by remembering that God's Word is about teaching us to love. Keeping love of God and neighbor before us can prevent us from getting so wrapped up in religion that we forget about God.

It is a common practice in some traditions to choose a discipline for the season of Lent. Rather than arbitrarily choosing something to give up or take on, perhaps we should first look at the unifying principle that guides us. If a practice doesn't teach us to love, we waste time with distractions that will never help us find God.

Lord, teach us to measure all revelations of you by using the bottom line of love.

Friday after Ash Wednesday

Deliver us from the presumption of coming to this Table
for solace only, and not for strength;
for pardon only, and not for renewal.
Let the grace of this Holy Communion
make us one body, one spirit in Christ,
that we may worthily serve the world in his name.

— Eucharistic Prayer C, p. 372

Many see the Christian way as one in which we behave a certain way in this life in order to earn an afterlife with God. It is no small wonder that this perception fails to draw people toward God and toward Christianity. It is difficult to make the case for a deity who demands sacrifice throughout this life in order to earn the prize of eternal life.

In Eucharistic Prayer C, we pray for God to "Deliver us from coming to this table for solace only, and not for strength; for pardon only, and not for renewal." That prayer highlights a dimension of Christian faith that is often forgotten: we don't follow Christ to earn eternal life after death, but to touch eternity during this life. God wants us to have life and to have it abundantly. That abundant, eternal life comes to us each time we choose to love God and neighbor.

Certainly we come to God asking for forgiveness of our sins. But the knowledge of God's forgiveness equips us, as disciples of Jesus, to forgive those who hurt us. We don't seek God's mercy for our own benefit alone, but to strengthen and renew us so that we can offer mercy to the next person. Knowledge of our own forgiveness and our value in God's sight equips us to love others—even those considered unlovable by human standards.

To live into our discipleship, we must come to God's table for solace and strength, for pardon and renewal. Our own healing prepares us to help others heal. Yes, as Christians, we do believe in life after death. But because of the strength and renewal we find in the Eucharist, we also believe in life before death.

Gracious God, open our eyes
to see the eternal in the now.

Saturday after Ash Wednesday

> *Will you continue in the apostles' teaching*
> *and fellowship, in the breaking of bread,*
> *and in the prayers?*
> *I will, with God's help.*

— The Baptismal Covenant, p. 304

When I moved from a rented apartment to a house, I suddenly faced many tasks I hadn't done before. I struggled at first, until I realized that my problems resulted from a scarcity of tools. No work can be done well without the proper tools.

We need the proper tools as we seek to be disciples of Jesus, too. Putting God at the center of our lives doesn't happen by magic. It isn't an easy task, even when our hearts truly intend and want alignment with God's will.

In the baptismal covenant, when we say that we will "continue in the apostles' teaching and fellowship, in the breaking of bread, and in the prayers," we're identifying tools for discipleship. Those tools come to us through our church tradition. "The apostles' teaching and fellowship" points to church history and tradition, toward all that the church and its members have done to carry Jesus' message faithfully.

We practice "the breaking of bread" each time we celebrate the Eucharist, the ritual shared meal in which we consume—and remember we are part of—the body of Christ. If we decide our participation in the Eucharist is a just another "should" or obligation, we miss the point. In the breaking of bread at Eucharist, we admit our own brokenness and accept the charge to help heal the world around us.

We put another tool—"the prayers"—to work when we pray regularly for one another, either privately or in worship together. Prayer isn't simply a pious wish list, but an acknowledgement that we are one body and that the well-being of one part of the body affects the health of us all.

So will we, by sharpening and engaging these tools, truly become disciples of the risen Christ?

We will, with God's help.

Give us humble hearts, O God,
to remember that we can love only with your help.

First Sunday of Lent

Gracious Father,
we pray for thy holy Catholic Church....
Where it is corrupt, purify it;
where it is in error, direct it;
where in any thing it is amiss, reform it.
Where it is right, strengthen it.

— Prayer for the Church, p. 816

Health-conscious consumers now demand fuller disclosure about calorie counts and other nutrition information on foods. Restaurants often resist providing this, fearing it could cost them customers.

For us as disciples, Lent offers the perfect time to ask what truly feeds us—physically, emotionally, and spiritually. Are we being fed by God or by religion? Have our spiritual lives become so familiar and routine that they no longer nourish us in healthy, vibrant ways?

The traditional approach of practicing spiritual discipline during Lent can help us identify which habits work and which do not. Giving something up may free time, energy, and focus in a surprising way. It may help us discover how much of ourselves we have invested in small, nonproductive habits.

We also may not realize that our well-intentioned spiritual practices no longer work to draw us nearer to God. Taking on a new or renewed spiritual discipline during Lent may teach us fresh and powerful ways of seeking and seeing God. We may find something previously unrecognized or untried that our souls have craved all along.

In our Prayer for the Church, we ask God to correct the church when it is wrong and strengthen it when it is right. Lent can help each of us take those same steps. Changing our ways of seeking God—whether by giving something up or taking something on—can bump us out of our comfort zones and bring fresh insight and energy. Such changes, taken on for this brief season, can teach us exactly what feeds us in body, mind, and soul. And Lent may be the ideal time to decide if the cost of our spiritual practices is greater than the nourishment they provide.

Loving God, help us use this season to renew our practice of faith.

Monday, First Week of Lent

*O God of peace, who has taught us
that in returning and rest we shall be saved,
in quietness and in confidence shall be our strength:
By the might of your Spirit lift us,
we pray, to your presence,
where we may be still and know that you are God.*

— Prayer for Quiet Confidence, p. 832

An anechoic chamber is an insulated room so quiet that it can disorient its occupants. The human body uses many cues—some based on sound—to achieve balance and physical movement. A perfectly quiet room unnerves our senses.

The human psyche also uses sound to achieve balance and movement in life. We take cues from others to determine our course. What will people say if we choose a way seen as countercultural? What voices will we hear within, telling us simply to go along with the way things are rather than asking questions? What questions will plague us, internally and externally, when we claim to hear God?

Most people today have little chance of finding a quiet place. Most of us aren't terribly sure that we even want such a place, afraid of what we might hear in the stillness. Like those in the quiet room, we become anxious in the absence of familiar sounds.

But being a disciple asks us to have the courage to seek the quiet—at least occasionally. In the Prayer for Quiet Confidence, we ask to be lifted into God's presence, where we may "be still, and know" God. True confidence needs regular, intentional intimacy with God, away from the chaos and the noise of our daily lives.

To do God's work, we have to find time to step away, into a room so quiet that we can hear our own heartbeat. If we can practice intentionally seeking that quiet, we may hear something we haven't heard in ages. We may hear the very voice of God.

God of peace, teach us to love the quiet.

Tuesday, First Week of Lent

*Glory to God whose power, working in us,
can do infinitely more than we can ask or imagine.*

— Daily Morning Prayer: Rite One, p. 60

When the first paperback books appeared in the United States in 1939, publishers thought the cheaper, less sturdy books would have little impact on the book market. Now, more than seventy years later, e-readers are shifting the market again, threatening the demand for any printed reading material at all.

In technology and in many aspects of everyday life, we have become accustomed to rapid change and adjustment. That ability to adapt makes me wonder why we have so much trouble believing that God acts in our lives in new ways. The Word of God—both printed and incarnate—remains alive, but often we're more comfortable regarding it as static.

At the close of Morning Prayer, we acknowledge that God's power "can do infinitely more than we can ask or imagine." But as disciples of the risen

Christ, do we live that way? Do we acknowledge God's continuing creative power? Or do we become so attached to our familiar ways of thinking about God that we remain stuck in one place?

"Disciples" and "discipline" come from the same root word, so our ways of following Jesus must have order and regularity. But regularity in practice can also plant seeds of complacency, preventing us from seeing God's continuing creation, both outside in the world and within our own hearts.

As we try to be faithful about following Jesus, it is easy to become too comfortable with our worship, prayer, and community. Lent gives us the opportunity to try new patterns. It offers the perfect framework—a brief trial period—for stepping out of our comfort zones.

What new revelation might God have for us if we surrender, even temporarily, our need to remain in a spiritual routine? What new Word from God might we understand if we bypass the form and focus on the substance?

Probably much more than we could ask or imagine.

> *God, open our hearts to new and surprising revelations of you.*

Wednesday, First Week of Lent

O God, by whose grace thy servant…
enkindled with the fire of thy love,
became a burning and a shining light in thy Church:
Grant that we also may be aflame
with the spirit of love and discipline,
and may ever walk before thee as children of light.

— Collect Of a Monastic, p. 198

Before every Olympic Games, millions of people watch a runner carry the Olympic torch to the Games' venue for the lighting of the Olympic flame. The scene evokes images of deities, and the torch harks back to Prometheus's theft of fire from the gods. In mythology, fire may have been one of the first symbols of divinity.

On the occasions when we remember the monastic tradition, we speak of such persons as "enkindled with the fire of thy love" to "become a burning and shining light in thy Church." That willingness to carry God's fire faithfully is even more important in the wider world. When we declare ourselves Christ's disciples, the people in our lives may measure the depth and authenticity of Christian tradition by our interactions with them. We must carry the fire faithfully if our hurting and often hostile world is to see the truth of the gospel.

As we work to deepen our relationship with God, we can find no better symbol for our efforts than fire. Fire burns away impurities. It offers warmth and light, two things necessary to all life. And just as fire does not diminish when shared, but multiplies, so does the shared love of God.

As we go forward in our Lenten journey, will we continue to carry that blessed torch, that gift of fire from the heavens? Will the disciplines and choices we explore during Lent help us to burn with heavenly desires so that we can continue to offer to others the Good News of God in Christ? Will we faithfully carry the fire that warms and lights the world?

Dear God, source of all light, give us the humility and strength to carry your fire faithfully to others.

Thursday, First Week of Lent

From all blindness of heart;
from pride, vainglory, and hypocrisy;
from envy, hatred, and malice;
and from all want of charity, Good Lord, deliver us.

— The Great Litany, p. 149

The field of extreme-value statistics investigates mathematics and probabilities involved in breaking records in sports, climatology, and other areas. As athletic records are broken less and less frequently, researchers wonder if the biomechanical limits of athletes are finally being approached.

We human beings love to believe that we have no limits, that we can solve any problem if given enough time and resources. And while following Christ gives us confidence in our gifts, we have to be careful not to slip into "blindness of heart… pride, [and] vainglory." Aware that we are forgiven, we can easily think that we need consult God only on matters that we have labeled "spiritual."

In truth, though, discipleship means that all matters are spiritual. Following Christ means doing as Christ did, and includes our interaction with others as well as regular prayer and reflection. If we seek God's counsel and help only when we run across something we can't master, we miss the opportunity to let God form us in God's image. The problems that prompt us to say, "Good Lord, deliver us" may be problems we never would have encountered if we had first gone to God in prayer.

We all like to think that—somehow and someday—we might set a new record, see new heights in athletic or intellectual accomplishment. But athletes probably don't want to hear that the limits of human athletic achievement may be within sight. They want to believe that, like those who have gone before, they can go "higher, faster, stronger."

Ultimately, though, every one of us finds a place of loss or challenge or fear which no amount of human effort can master. In sports or in spiritual understanding, we can only go so far. But if we pray regularly for God's counsel and guidance, we can bring the kingdom of God to earth.

God, remind us that, with you, we can do all things.

Friday, First Week of Lent

You formed us in your own image,
giving the whole world into our care,
so that, in obedience to you, our Creator,
we might rule and serve all your creatures.
When our disobedience took us far from you,
you did not abandon us to the power of death.
In your mercy you came to our help,
so that in seeking you we might find you.

— Eucharistic Prayer D, p. 373

Evolutionary biologists have worked for decades to determine how birds first took flight. In simplest terms, some believe tree-dwellers fell into flying, while others believe ground dwellers flapped developing wings to go from ground to sky.

Christians entertain a similar debate about human origins and human fallibility. Some say we went from the sky to the ground, made originally in God's image but led astray through our free will and hubris. Others maintain that we went from ground to sky, beginning as depraved creatures who ultimately sought God.

While I enjoy such theological debate, my main task as a Christian is learning how to love in this time and place. Theology alone won't tell me how to place God at the center of my life. Theology alone cannot give me the strength to love those I do not like. Theology alone cannot get me through the dark nights of loss and fear.

To answer such persistent questions, we need to work not only on theology, but also on the spirituality of our everyday lives. What disciplines can we practice that will allow us to live in God's image and reflect God's will? What practices can we undertake to place love—in other words, God—first in our ordinary lives?

Theology matters, but only with respect to its contribution to our relationship with God and with others. So did we go from sky to ground or from ground to sky? I have no idea. I do know that when I seek God faithfully, I can touch both heaven and earth.

Lord, give us the grace and humility
to flourish in both earth and sky.

Saturday, First Week of Lent

Almighty God, to you all hearts are open,
all desires known, and from you no secrets are hid:
Cleanse the thoughts of our hearts by the inspiration
of your Holy Spirit, that we may perfectly love you,
and worthily magnify your holy Name;
through Christ our Lord.

— Collect for Purity, p. 355

An article on home health and safety recommends unlocking the front door when you call 911 in a health emergency. That way, rescuers can get in even when you are incapacitated.

Such advice certainly makes sense; few would argue with it when life and death are on the line. And yet we do not understand the same concept with regard to God. We pray to God, but then God cannot fully reach us because the front door to our hearts remains locked. Perhaps that tendency explains why we open our Eucharistic celebration with the Collect for Purity, which says to God, "to you all hearts are open, all desires known, and from you no secrets are hid: Cleanse the thoughts of our hearts by the inspiration of your Holy Spirit."

This Lenten season, we would do well to listen carefully and take the Collect for Purity to heart. We strengthen our worship and our faith if we truly mean it when we say to God that our hearts are open. Do we just mouth these words each Sunday, or do we mean for our participation in the body of Christ to transform us into loving human beings? We need to hear those words we say so routinely and truly invite God in to change us.

We cannot become disciples if we call on God to save us, but keep our hearts closed by our failure to forgive, our criticism, and prejudice. After all, what's the point in calling for help if we won't allow help inside the door?

> *God, open us to your true*
> *and deep transformation.*

Second Sunday of Lent

Fountain of life and source of all goodness,
you made all things and fill them with your blessing;
you created them to rejoice
in the splendor of your radiance.

— Eucharistic Prayer D, p. 373

Near my office, I watched the construction of a new bank building. After the preliminary framing, the first part of the building constructed was the bank's vault. It was clear from the very beginning that the vault represented the essence of the building's purpose.

In our spiritual lives, we rarely have the luxury of starting from scratch, of determining the core of what we do so that everything else can be built around it. Our lives grow in many directions, stretched thin by conflicting priorities, demands, and relationships. Rather than beginning with the vault, most of us build and fill countless other aspects of life and then try to place God in the center.

Eucharistic Prayer D offers a statement of the vault of Christian faith, the essence of what we do in our faith lives. In the prayer, we say, "Fountain of life and source of all goodness, you made all things and fill them with your blessing." We go on to say, "You created them to rejoice in the splendor of your radiance."

Those words tell us that God alone should be found in the innermost vault, the heart of the disciple. Remembering God as the "fountain of life and source of all goodness" means that God remains at the center of life. No earthly harm can come to a person whose life flows from the knowledge and love of God in Christ.

Today, and every day of our lives, even the most faithful and disciplined follower of Jesus Christ will navigate a life filled with demands. But we can fully and passionately seek God armed with this key guideline: We have to remember to build the vault first.

God, let all priorities in our lives
flow from the fountain of your goodness.

Monday, Second Week of Lent

For these and all other sins which I cannot now remember, I am truly sorry.

— The Reconciliation of a Penitent, p. 447

Medical science has vastly improved diagnostic techniques and therapies for cancer, but techniques for cancer surgery have changed more slowly. Recently though, scientists developed a way to make cancer cells glow, so that surgeons can see what to remove and what to leave untouched.

In human life, much of what offends God is ignored—or even glorified—by human society. We can remain blissfully unaware that we have taken up habits or accepted circumstances dissonant with the way of Christ. Often, we don't change because we miss those dissonances within ourselves and in our lives. We might do better if something could make the disease within us glow, helping us to distinguish what is healthy from what is not.

In the rite of reconciliation, we acknowledge that we cannot always see faults within ourselves.

We seek forgiveness for particular sins that we can name, but also for "all other sins which I cannot now remember."

This Lenten season, as we practice the disciple's way, changing our habits may help bring the disease within us to light. Our Lenten practices may identify places in our lives that bring us down and prevent our being more fully with God.

We must learn to walk in the tension of being aware of our sin without beating up on ourselves. If we focus too much on our own past sins, we will not be able to find the energy and grace to move forward. But if we make intentional errors, knowing we will be forgiven, we skim the surface with no deep sense of grace and forgiveness.

While we are well aware of the sin within us most of the time, many forms of selfishness—of sin—remain glorified by our individualistic society. I often wish that the sins which I "cannot now remember" would light up so I could see them clearly. Then I would know for certain what to remove and what to leave untouched.

Lord God, let your light
reveal the sources of our disquiet.

Tuesday, Second Week of Lent

O God…we humbly beseech you graciously to behold and bless those whom we love, now absent from us. Defend them from all dangers of soul and body.

— Collect for the Absent, p. 830

In recent years, the nation of Guatemala has become so dominated by violence and corruption that many have wondered how it could ever change. Then, for some reason, one particular shooting finally spurred protesters and government reformers to take action.

What prompts human action in such circumstances? When does the human spirit say "Enough!" and move to change—rather than accept—the way things are?

In this age of information overload, it takes a dramatic turn of events to grab our attention. Many good, compassionate people are moved to help in times of acute crises like natural disasters, horrible accidents, or untimely deaths. We are less likely, though, to pay attention to those who routinely live in want, danger, or strife.

Jesus often scandalized those around him by noticing the marginalized, drawing them near, and helping them find healing and wholeness. As disciples of Christ, we, too, are expected to have eyes for the invisible and ears for the voiceless. By praying the Collect for the Absent, we can remember that we are to love not only those who make headlines, but also those who simply struggle, every ordinary day, to get by.

Such invisible people are "those whom we love, now absent from us." Physically, they live all around us, but they are absent from our thoughts and our calls to action. Perhaps during Lent, we can turn our attention less to the acute and more to the chronic problems in our culture.

Most of us are generous enough in spirit to respond to acute crises in our society and the world. But when will we become so immersed in Christ's way that we become interested in righting wrongs that don't make headlines? Will we ever become so Christ-like that we remember to love those who are "now absent from us"?

Patient Lord, teach us to see those previously invisible to us.

Wednesday, Second Week of Lent

*Sacraments sustain our present hope
and anticipate its future fulfillment.*

— The Catechism, p. 861

Once, a song I'd never heard before brought tears to my eyes. I had no idea what the lyrics meant—and I still don't—but I am still deeply moved each time I hear this song.

In our Episcopal tradition, liturgy holds the power to move us in the same deep, mysterious way. Based on Scripture and church tradition, it connects us to God at a level we cannot articulate or fully recognize. According to the Catechism in *The Book of Common Prayer*, the "sacraments sustain our present hope and anticipate its future fulfillment." They are not incorporated into worship as mere symbols, but to move our souls to resonate with that "present hope and future fulfillment" of faith in Jesus Christ.

As disciples, we expressly invite the presence of God into our lives. Once we make that honest invitation, we relinquish control over the times and ways God will speak to us. During the season of Lent, we experience the liturgies for specific days: Ash Wednesday, Palm Sunday, Maundy Thursday, Good Friday, the Easter Vigil, and Easter Sunday. Almost certainly, the words and sacramental acts of one or more of those services will move us powerfully, perhaps even to tears. We can repress those tears, determined to experience these liturgies as symbols, or we can allow them to transport us to that place of present hope and future fulfillment.

Being a disciple of Jesus means letting go of personal agendas and personal destinations and simply following. That choice takes us to places that are sometimes frightening, unnerving, and yes, places of tears. Will we allow God to move us this day, this season? Will we surrender our need to be in control and allow the deep messages of the liturgy to resonate within us? Will we let God's music move us to tears and see where those tears will take us?

God, give us the courage to be moved to tears.

Thursday, Second Week of Lent

Almighty and most merciful God,
kindle within us the fire of love,
that by its cleansing flame we may be purged
of all our sins and made worthy
to worship you in spirit and in truth.

— An Order of Worship for the Evening, p. 111

Once, when I was a child, my dad gathered up tree limbs and other trash on our property and began to burn them. But when the wind pushed the fire into our pasture, he had to call the fire department for help in getting the fire back under control.

When we call ourselves disciples of Jesus Christ, don't we fear a similar fate? Aren't we afraid that if we truly live as God calls us to live, we will give up control and habits and relationships precious to us? We often pray for God to change us, but our hearts add the silent footnote, "But not too much."

In Lent, we often make small, temporary changes that we can control. We prefer to build small, nonthreatening fires that we can manage. But to be true disciples of Christ asks us to invite the fire without trying to control it. Following Christ means opening ourselves to significant change, so we can be "purged of all our sins and made worthy to worship" God. It takes great courage—and deep trust in God—to let that "cleansing flame" start within us without becoming anxious about losing control.

We surrender certain habits and take on disciplines during Lent to gather and burn the rubbish that obstructs our view of God and also of our authentic selves. What will it take for us to go all in, to allow that fire to go where it will? Do we have the courage to invite true, deep change, knowing that God's fire may threaten or destroy something dear to us? Or will we remain content with our manageable little fires?

Almighty God, kindle in us the fire of love, and let its cleansing flame go where you will.

Friday, Second Week of Lent

*In corporate worship, we unite ourselves
with others to acknowledge the holiness of God,
to hear God's Word, to offer prayer,
and to celebrate the sacraments.*

— The Catechism, p. 857

The arrival of tourists can spell disaster for an area. Economies benefit from tourism, but visitors can also introduce new diseases and plants and animals damaging to the environment.

Human life spent in pursuit of God often takes place in a similar tension. Seeking to duplicate or deepen our experiences of God, we may take up habits that actually inhibit the very thing we seek. If we become complacent with liturgy and other spiritual tools, that complacency can damage rather than enhance intimacy with God.

As Christians, we believe that we are saved by God and not by our own actions. But if we need not—and cannot—earn salvation, it's a short step to thinking we have no obligation to God.

In worship, we come together to help one another avoid the temptations of complacency and arrogance. The catechism tells us that "we unite ourselves with others to acknowledge the holiness of God, to hear God's Word, to offer prayer, and to celebrate the sacraments." We have to come together regularly to remind each other of the holiness of God and the unspeakable gift of God's grace.

During Lent and in all of Christian life, disciples walk a fine line. While we seek God in regular worship, we have to avoid the idea that we can control or domesticate God for our own use. Spiritual practice helps us live in that tension, where God is accessible yet outside of our control.

We all want to create spiritual environments where we can experience God deeply and regularly. But we must never believe that we have tamed God's power. We cannot allow the carelessness of tourists to destroy the habitats that nurture God's presence in our lives.

God, give us wisdom to nurture
our relationship with you
while honoring your sovereignty.

Saturday, Second Week of Lent

*Grant, O God, that your holy and life-giving Spirit
may so move every human heart…that barriers which
divide us may crumble, suspicions disappear,
and hatreds cease; that our divisions being healed,
we may live in justice and peace.*

— Collect for Social Justice, p. 823

Much of the world still lives in the shadow of the dangerous climate created by Soviet leader Joseph Stalin. He purposefully created a series of states designed to foment divisiveness and prevent a unified country. Millions live with the legacy of the resulting ethnic and national tension.

Stalin knew that with unity comes the power to overcome untold oppression, a lesson that holds true not only with nations, but within individual human beings as well. If a person tries to juggle too many priorities, all of them will suffer. At some point, one aspect of life goes to war with another and priorities fight for control of physical, emotional, and spiritual resources.

So divided loyalties not only cause unrest for political states, but also for human hearts. Unless we decide to put God alone at the center of our lives, we will remain in conflict, driving ourselves crazy in the effort to make everything a top priority. The Lenten season is the ideal time to clear out the noise in our hearts and focus so clearly on God that all priorities flow from that center.

Perhaps for this short season, we can deepen discipleship by regaining our focus on God. We can examine priorities, resources, and choices, putting God first, rather than pretending we are victimized by our schedules and priorities.

We have the power to put God at the center and stop the warring factions within our hearts, minds, and schedules. And when God's Spirit truly inhabits our hearts, barriers that divide us crumble, and our divisions being healed, we live in justice and peace. Finding union with God, though, first requires finding it within ourselves.

Lord, bring us the peace of single-mindedness.

Third Sunday of Lent

For those who do not yet believe,
and for those who have lost their faith,
that they may receive the light of the Gospel,
we pray to you, O Lord.

— Prayers of the People, Form V, p. 390

Architecture meets environmentalism in houses that rotate to take full advantage of the sun's rays. Now highly-developed, the technology results in homes that generate up to five times the energy they consume. The approach makes great sense spiritually as well as architecturally. Rather than lamenting a loss of light—an awareness of God—why can't we discipline ourselves to seek that light, to turn continually so that we remain keenly aware of God's presence?

A person who chooses to be a disciple of Christ proclaims a willingness to seek the light rather than curse the darkness. We have to realize, though, that every human being faces difficult and dark times when it seems impossible to find the light.

Enduring such times does not mean we are unfaithful; it simply means that we are human.

In the Prayers of the People, we pray "for those who do not yet believe, and for those who have lost their faith, that they may receive the light of the Gospel." Such prayers are not just offered for those who cannot muster the strength to seek God; they apply to each one of us. In any given moment, when our weakness, despair, or fear have blocked the light, we might be among those who lack belief or who have lost their faith. We pray for the strength and the faith to help others when their faith weakens, and we hope that others will pray for us and help us when our own faith falters.

As disciples of Christ, we are dwelling places for the most high God. But the corners and recesses of our modest dwelling places cannot receive that holy light without our concerted and faithful efforts to turn, continually, toward it.

*Lord, let every person we meet
see that our hearts are turned to you.*

Monday, Third Week of Lent

Through Jesus Christ our Lord;
who was tempted in every way as we are,
yet did not sin.
By his grace we are able to triumph over every evil.

— Preface for Lent, p. 379

Years ago, filmmakers came to my hometown to make a movie, filming part of it across the street from my office. Many of us got word that the stars were there, so we went over, hoping to catch a glimpse of someone famous. It's the sort of thing we all do sometimes, hoping to see or speak with someone of note. But in our wildest dreams, do we ever imagine that we could actually glimpse God in human flesh?

The incarnation of God among us is the most priceless gift of our Christian tradition. In other times and faiths, humankind felt the understandable need to imagine something or someone "out there" to give hope and to explain the inexplicable.

But how did we progress from the idea of God as Creator to the idea of God as personal savior? How in the world do we, even as Christians, remember that God "up there" became God down here?

Even more stunning than incarnation—and more comforting—is the idea that God in human flesh "was tempted in every way as we are, yet did not sin." The Lord Jesus Christ did not live up there somewhere, removed from the mess of us little people. Jesus lived here, with us, in a real world filled with pain, fatigue, and even temptation.

Given the gift of incarnation in our tradition, how do we, as Christ's disciples, respond? We imitate Jesus, stopping to listen, touching those considered untouchable, forgiving those who would hurt or even kill us. When we live as faithful disciples, doing our best to live the life Jesus modeled, we draw others to him. After all, who wouldn't show up, hoping to catch a glimpse of God at work within us and among us?

God, let our every action point toward you.

Tuesday, Third Week of Lent

*Walk in love, as Christ loved us
and gave himself for us,
an offering and sacrifice to God.*

— The Holy Eucharist: Rite Two, p. 376

Often in my life, I've embarrassed myself by mispronouncing words. I read a great deal, and sometimes get crazy ideas about how words actually sound. When our processing of knowledge is strictly internal and personal, we can make mistakes in both spoken and spiritual language. Our ideas about God need to be developed in community to avoid those internal mistakes.

The key "word" we humans mispronounce is the Word of God incarnate. We speak of God, often portraying God in ways which suit our own needs. But by remaining in community with one another, sharing our joys and burdens, we say the word "God" aloud and we learn from one another that its meaning is love.

In the liturgy we bring our gifts to the altar, often preceded by the words, "Walk in love, as

Christ loved us and gave himself for us, an offering and sacrifice to God." With these words—and in all our communal worship, outreach work, study, and prayer—we remind each other that our primary gift to God is to love. If we do not participate in Christian community, we risk misconstruing God's incarnate Word, remaking it to fit our own agendas.

Many believe that they can worship God well without participating in a church community—and if our hearts were perfectly formed in Christ's image, we might be able to back such a claim. But without regular reminders from other Christians about the true, loving nature of God, we are in danger of hearing only what we want to hear.

Christian community, done correctly, offers us both unconditional love and accountability. Left to process our ideas internally, every one of us may stray into convenient and inaccurate ways of understanding God. But saying our ideas aloud to one another makes it more likely that the thoughts of our hearts truly point to a God of love.

> *Lord Jesus, give us the humility*
> *to keep each other accountable.*

Wednesday, Third Week of Lent

Will you strive for justice and peace among all people, and respect the dignity of every human being?

— The Baptismal Covenant, p. 305

More and more, our society minimizes and even eliminates the human factor in its functions. In everything from checkout lines to warplanes, we involve fewer human beings. The unfortunate result can be seeing people as nothing more than part of the machinery of our economy.

In our most basic ritual—baptism—we practice seeing God in one another. When asked in the baptismal covenant, "Will you strive for justice and peace among all people, and respect the dignity of every human being," it requires little effort to promise to help the person being baptized or our neighbor in the pew. But outside of church, it is frighteningly easy to see people in their jobs, their cars, or in other roles as nothing more than machinery.

The willingness and ability to see human beings as individuals remains the most striking aspect of Jesus' earthly life. Often, when asked for help, he stopped what he was doing, setting his own agenda aside to see and hear an individual marginalized by society. For instance, in the Gospel of Mark, Jesus' followers tried to keep the blind man Bartimaeus from delaying Jesus on his way. But Mark tells us that "Jesus stood still, and said, 'Call him here,'" then healed the man of his blindness (Mark 10:46-52).

As modern-day disciples of Christ, we have to work very intentionally to see every human being we encounter. The pace of life today encourages us to hurry past, get where we're going, grab what we need, and move on. But that pace requires us to ignore others' needs, especially the need to be seen and heard, embraced and healed.

Ironically, we followers of Christ can find ourselves in a hurry to get to a commitment or activity involving church or religion. Yet placing religious priorities ahead of the basic needs of a human being ignores not only that person but also the example and teaching of Jesus. When we sign on to follow Christ, our agendas must change to make room for the love of God and others. We cannot hurry through life and still respect the dignity of every human being.

God, give us eyes truly to see every human being.

Thursday, Third Week of Lent

Lord Jesus, stay with us,
for evening is at hand and the day is past;
be our companion in the way, kindle our hearts,
and awaken hope, that we may know you as you are
revealed in Scripture and the breaking of bread.
Grant this for the sake of your love.

— Collect for the Presence of Christ, p. 124

The first night after moving from a one-story upstairs apartment to a two-story house, I admit I experienced a bit of fear. My old apartment had only one entrance, so my imagination went wild with the knowledge that a would-be intruder now had four doors and numerous large, ground-floor windows for access.

As disciples of Jesus, we cannot be effective if we live in fear. We cannot accept the forgiveness and tender love of God if we have closed ourselves off in an effort to protect ourselves. And we certainly cannot show compassion, exulting and weeping with others, if we insist on living behind tightly closed doors.

Opening ourselves to the prospect of loving God and neighbor means opening ourselves to a much wider spectrum of pain. To be loving, we must also be vulnerable, and that vulnerability will frighten us when our own nighttime comes. But the Good News of Christ is that our following him is only half the story.

The other side of choosing to follow Christ is that Christ also chooses to follow us. God stays with us, "when evening is at hand." God, through Jesus, is "our companion in the way." The lights may be turned off around us, but carrying Jesus with us promises to "kindle our hearts, and awaken hope." God lives in us, a light in the darkness, a comfort when we hear things that go bump in the night. Lord Jesus stays with us always—no matter how many doors and windows are left open on the ground floor.

Loving God, teach us to trust you so completely that we can open all the doors of our hearts.

Friday, Third Week of Lent

And, that we might live no longer for ourselves...
he sent the Holy Spirit,
his own first gift for those who believe,
to complete his work in the world.

— Eucharistic Prayer D, p. 374

Like most people, I have joked about using the word "practice" to describe the work of doctors and lawyers, even experienced ones. It's a bit unnerving to seek critical medical or legal help from someone who is still practicing. And yet, it is the best possible word to describe a Christian who actively seeks God. We court danger and arrogance when we use phrases like real Christian or true Christian to describe those who are serious about their Christian spirituality.

Choosing to be disciples of Christ means that we live our human lives keenly aware of our own imperfection. We are called to imitate Christ in loving God and others, but encumbered by human fear, selfishness, and doubt, we simply cannot love as perfectly as Jesus did. Still, we choose to try, because we know that the Holy Spirit, God's "own first gift to those who believe," empowers us to help bring about the kingdom of God.

Why don't we stop, admitting that we can never reach the goal of being like Christ, of loving others unconditionally? Rarely are we able, in other dimensions of our lives, to persevere in pursuing impossible goals. We lower our expectations or find another pursuit, one in which we can succeed. Why is this imitation of Christ different?

The answer, perhaps, is that we are not engaged in a human endeavor, but a divine one. Created in God's image, we long to be with God and like God. But free will also means we make imperfect choices. We strive to be people who "live no longer for ourselves," but sometimes we just aren't very good at it. That's why we call ourselves practicing Christians.

Most holy God,
give us the perseverance to imitate Christ,
no matter how feeble our efforts
may look in our own eyes.

Saturday, Third Week of Lent

*O God, the source of eternal light:
Shed forth your unending day upon us
who watch for you.*

— Collect for Saturdays, p. 123

I love this time of year, when we approach Daylight Saving Time again. While we adjust clocks and speak of the event as a "time change," I long for it because of the light change. We human beings go to great lengths to extend the day when possible and to light the darkness when it ends.

In the service of Evening Prayer, we ask God to "Shed forth your unending day upon us who watch for you." Nighttime, after all, can bring uncertainty, nameless fear, and anxiety. But in spiritual terms as well as chronological systems, the change we seek fits more into the category of light change than time change. We do not necessarily want to wish away the hours between dusk and dawn; we simply want to navigate those hours without fear.

The request in our prayers for "unending day" speaks of the eternal. We need to be reminded that God remains with us always, in darkness and in light. We need to be reminded that the power of God cannot be vanquished or even diminished by forces pressuring us here on earth. So we long not for unending physical light, but a constant awareness that God is here.

God created our souls to experience the eternal, even in the midst of the temporal. When we ask for God's "unending day," we are seeking the strength to weather life's challenges and to help others see light in the darkness. We don't want longer days to give us more time; we want them so we can experience more light. If we can practice focusing on the eternal over the temporal during Lent and all of life's seasons, we live in God's unending day. And we lead those around us to more than a time change—to a light change.

Lord Jesus Christ, be our light in the darkness.

Fourth Sunday of Lent

Gracious Father, whose blessed Son Jesus Christ
came down from heaven to be the true bread
which gives life to the world:
Evermore give us this bread,
that he may live in us, and we in him.

— Collect for the Fourth Sunday in Lent, p. 219

In the Greek pantheon, the god Hermes serves as the god of transitions and boundaries. While we serve the one true God and not one god among many, we find many boundaries crossed in the God of Jesus Christ.

Jesus' incarnation represents the key boundary-crossing in our faith tradition. In the Collect for the Fourth Sunday in Lent, we remember that crossing-over when we pray, "Gracious Father, whose blessed Son Jesus Christ came down from heaven to be the true bread which gives life to the world." We acknowledge that we cannot be sustained by human, earthly bread, and that the nourishment Jesus brings means that "he may live in us, and we in him."

So what does it mean, in the everyday life of a disciple, that God crossed the boundary between heaven and earth, between the human and the divine? Is it simply a display of God's love, or does it also empower our lives as human beings?

When we pray in the collect that "he may live in us, and we in him," we seek the courage and power to cross those boundaries ourselves. If our Lenten journey and all of the Christian way transforms us, then we find ways to love others as Jesus loved. We find ways to forgive others, even those who would have us killed, as Jesus forgave. We find ways to hear God's voice above the human din, as Jesus did.

In such moments, however brief, Jesus lives in us and works through us. And with our hearts open to deep transformation, we connect heaven to earth and the divine to human. For we worship the Lord Jesus Christ, the ultimate God of transitions and boundary-crossings.

Lord, inspire us to erase boundaries,
that we all may be one.

Monday, Fourth Week of Lent

"Do this for the remembrance of me."

— Eucharistic Prayer A, p. 362

My dad had the quickest wit of anyone I've met, and I often recount his jokes and comebacks with others. Telling those stories, I laugh and cry at the same time, delighted over his wit and longing for his presence. In trading stories about my dad, all of us who loved him remember him, finding ourselves in his presence again. Though physically gone, he is spiritually present in a powerful way. Our love for him means that he continues to live on in us—in the joy, words, and tenderness he invokes in us.

Our Eucharistic prayers reflect the same kind of remembering that invokes the presence of a loved one. They hold more power though, than the simple memory. Such remembering restores the body of Christ on earth, and every person who chooses to love becomes part of that body of believers.

In the Eucharistic prayer, we recall Jesus' instruction to "Do this for the remembrance of me." In those words, Jesus asks us to do much more than leaf through the memory album. He asks us to make him present to others by living as he lived.

Each time we love without thought of reward or condition, and each time we forgive others for having hurt us, we bring Christ's body to life again. When we hold the hand of a grieving or fearful friend, we become the hands of Christ, doing God's healing work in the world. When we speak words of forgiveness in response to those who have hurt us, we become the voice of Christ. When we invite others to lean on us, we become the shoulders of Christ, helping to bear the burdens of human existence. When we see the value in every human being, we become the eyes of Christ, looking with tenderness upon his beloved. In all physical gestures of human kindness, compassion, and care, we embody the presence of God on earth, "remembering" the body of Christ in human flesh.

The words and actions we share at Holy Eucharist hold great power, not only in creating memories, but in reassembling the body of Jesus Christ. Because we love him and because we imitate him in our compassion, forgiveness, and self-sacrifice for others, Jesus lives on. As disciples of Jesus Christ, we don't simply remember him, we re-member him.

> *Lord Jesus, energize our words*
> *and worship with your presence.*

Tuesday, Fourth Week of Lent

*Almighty God, we give you thanks
for surrounding us, as daylight fades,
with the brightness of the vesper light.*

— An Order of Worship for the Evening, p. 110

A town in the Italian Alps rests so deeply in a valley that it receives very little sunlight from November through February. To remedy the problem, its leaders decided to place a huge mirror on a hillside, three thousand feet up, to reflect sunlight into the village.

Every human being, even the most faithful, spends time in valleys so deep that the light cannot reach them. Even with a strong faith in the Resurrection, we struggle in times of loss or failure. When we lose hope or wrestle with doubt, we feel exiled in a valley that cannot be reached by light in any form.

Every person who chooses to follow Christ spends some time in valleys and some on mountaintops. We worship and pray and work in community so that we can support one another in difficult times. In one person's time of loss, fear, or doubt, other disciples take their places on the mountainside to reflect the light of God into the deep valleys.

In the Order of Worship for the Evening, we thank God for, "surrounding us, as the daylight fades, with the brightness of the vesper light." But the strength we seek in that vesper light doesn't appear magically to those in the valley; it shines through the tender care of others, offered in the name of God.

Like the village buried in the valley's deep darkness, Lent can sometimes feel like a dim place. In it, as in other times of waiting, we offer each other God's strength in simple human kindnesses. We make contact with one another regularly. We remind each other continually of the grace of God. We help one another remember that even death has been vanquished by the Resurrection of our Lord Jesus Christ. In other words, when one of us experiences darkness, another disciple becomes the mirror on the hillside.

Lord, let our lives reflect your light into the valleys.

Wednesday, Fourth Week of Lent

Holy and gracious Father…you, in your mercy,
sent Jesus Christ, your only and eternal Son,
to share our human nature,
to live and die as one of us,
to reconcile us to you,
the God and Father of all.

— Eucharistic Prayer A, p. 362

The United States' space program began sending missions into space in the late 1950s. But it took almost twenty-five years for the program to design a space vehicle that could not only take off, but also land safely enough to be reused on successive missions. The landing—not the launching—presented the greater challenge.

If we choose to be disciples of Christ, we will certainly experience the highs of intimate encounters with God. But we cannot live in the high places. We have to find ways to bring the inspiration and passion of these experiences into our everyday lives. God does not give them to us to wear like a badge, a reminder of the day we were allowed to touch the sky.

We are asked to follow Jesus Christ as the one human being who loved perfectly, who translated the perfect love of God into the human experience. We remember that incarnation in much of our prayer and worship, but especially in the Eucharistic prayers. There we narrate the story of the incarnation, saying, "You, in your mercy, sent your only and eternal Son, to share our human nature, to live and die as one of us."

God lived among us to show how it looks when God lives within us. If we are allowed to ascend the mountain to be with God, our human nature attempts to spurn life in the valley. But Jesus Christ came to live with us, to show us how human flesh looks when enlivened and inspired by the presence of divinity. We are then called to allow divinity to inspire us to live among humanity. And once again, the landing—not the launching—presents the more difficult challenge.

God within us, allow us to live in a way that brings heaven to earth.

Thursday, Fourth Week of Lent

*That it may please thee to give us a heart
to love and fear thee,
and diligently to live after thy commandments,
We beseech thee to hear us, good Lord.*

— The Great Litany, p. 150

In political campaigns, the candidate takes center stage, giving speeches and experiencing wins and losses. But there are all manner of people, critical to the effort, behind the scenes of every campaign: polling consultants, fundraisers, opposition researchers, and countless others.

Likewise, everyone who speaks as a Christian needs to do significant work offstage, in the back rooms, and in the field. If we try to talk about God without doing the background work, we will never help win a soul for Christ. In fact, it is because of self-aggrandizing people who claim to know all about God's will and God's ways that many people reject Christianity. Untold numbers, hungry for spirituality, refuse to explore Christianity because they have seen Christians use Scripture as a self-serving weapon instead of a way to know God.

In The Great Litany, we beseech God to grant "That it may please thee to give us a heart to love and fear thee, and diligently to live after thy commandments." As disciples of Christ, how do we nurture that desire to "diligently live after" God's commandments? How do we stop twisting Jesus' words and story to fit our own needs and agendas, and truly follow him?

We find the answer in the back rooms of our hearts. There we identify, honestly, our bottom line as disciples of Christ. If our goal is to wear God like a badge, we will not succeed any more than a political candidate who is all form and no substance. If our goal mirrors the essence of God—love—then we have done the work to find "a heart to love thee." Only when we love, will others elect to explore Christianity.

Loving God, give us the strength and courage
to do the work of nurturing your presence within us.

Friday, Fourth Week of Lent

Rend your hearts and not your garments.
Return to the Lord your God,
for he is gracious and merciful,
slow to anger and abounding in steadfast love,
and repents of evil.

— Joel 2:13, Daily Morning Prayer: Rite Two, p. 76

As a competitive child who loved games and sports, I especially hated losing to someone who didn't play by the rules. My parents told me that cheaters never prosper, but life experience has taught me otherwise. People who lie, cheat, and victimize others prosper all the time.

Selfish and malicious forces often win out in our culture. As disciples of Jesus, we know that we find intimacy with God when we make good and moral choices, and we struggle to convince others of the importance of making such choices. But the apparent flourishing of evil frustrates the case for living good and godly lives.

Doesn't each of us—even the most faithful—wonder why the forces of evil seem to rule the world while the power of good waits outside the door? And on a less cosmic scale, we know that God's favor cannot be earned, yet we can slip into believing that those we name as evil should be excluded from God's favor. But we fail to live life abundantly if we spend our time lamenting the success of others, no matter how selfish or evil they may be.

In these words, read at Morning Prayer during Lent, the prophet Joel tells us, "Rend your hearts and not your garments. Return to the Lord your God." That admonition reminds us allow ourselves to be transformed inwardly, so that people around us will see that we, as disciples of Christ, practice what we preach.

We are human, and we can't help sometimes hoping that people will get what they deserve. But God asks disciples to love others—even those who don't play by the rules.

Lord, teach us to be slow to anger
and abounding in love.

Saturday, Fourth Week of Lent

That it may please thee to give to all people increase of grace to hear and receive thy Word, and to bring forth the fruits of the Spirit.

— The Great Litany, p. 150

Some nations have reduced both prison populations and crime rates by using noncustodial sentences, penalties that do not involve prison time. The noncustodial approach seems counterintuitive, though. How can we discourage crime if criminals aren't afraid of losing their freedom?

The idea that only fear can inspire discipline represents the greatest enemy to the human understanding of grace. Many believe that we remain in God's favor only as long as we live virtuous lives. After all, won't sin flourish if people don't fear punishment?

For the disciple of Christ, moral behavior comes not from fear, but from gratitude. In the Great Litany, we beseech God, "That it may please thee to give to all people increase of grace to hear and receive thy Word, and to bring forth the fruits of the Spirit." Such prayers remind us that we try to live good and moral lives not because we fear punishment, but because we want to share the abundant life we have found in Christ. Social justice, morality, compassion, and loving kindness are not motivated by fear, but by gratitude for God's freeing us from sin.

After all, if we believe that we find intimacy with God and eternal life because of our actions, haven't we made the cross of Jesus Christ irrelevant? As believers in salvation through our Lord Jesus Christ, we have to remember continually that we are saved by the grace of God, and not by our own actions. And when we live by that good news and share it with others, we see grace increase in our hearts and theirs.

Lord, let our gratitude
free us from the prison of fear.

Fifth Sunday of Lent

*The blessing of God Almighty, the Father,
the Son, and the Holy Spirit,
be upon you and remain with you for ever.*

— The Holy Eucharist: Rite One, p. 339

I suspect most Christians struggle intellectually with the concept of the Holy Trinity. We believe in one God, but we invoke "Father, Son, and Holy Spirit" in countless places in our liturgy. The Trinity allows us to see different facets of God and the different ways that God works in human life.

I once preferred to see God exclusively as the Father, a power above us. Though my own human father was not a disciplinarian, some of my earliest adult ideas of God included a father's discipline. Much of our Christian tradition seems to equate the "Father" aspect of the Trinity with the law, giving us the intimidating disciplinarian who keeps us out of trouble.

Later in life, I preferred to think of God as the Son, the very being of God in human flesh. Seeing God incarnate in Jesus allowed me to have a more practical faith, one which translated the power of God into acts of human flesh. God the Son gave me tangible ways of putting God's presence into practice, as Jesus showed me how a perfect human being responds to the challenges of earthly existence.

I struggled most to understand God the Holy Spirit. My struggle came not from the inability to see God changing me and working within me, but from the "bad press" given to the Holy Spirit by friends. Once I realized that my fear of the Holy Spirit came from the flawed ideas I'd been given, I loved the idea that God's presence lives in me and works through me.

Ultimately, I see the Trinity as constant and as important in a maturing and more complete view of God. I have moved from God the Father and disciplinarian, to God the Son and model human being, to God the Holy Spirit and the power of God at work within us.

God above us. God with us. God in us.
God, protect us, walk with us, inspire us.

Monday, Fifth Week of Lent

Bless the lands and waters,
and multiply the harvests of the world…
that our land may give her increase;
and save us from selfish use of what thou givest.

— For the Harvest of Lands and Waters, p. 828

Some legends suggest that we call the Promised Land "the land of milk and honey" because milk and honey are rare foods, in that nothing dies to produce them. Won't we truly find paradise—heaven on earth—when the things that fill one human being do not mean emptiness for another? As the world operates now, generally one loses so another can gain. For example, for one person to enjoy advanced technology at low prices, another must work for deplorably low wages.

In our prayer For the Harvest of Lands and Waters, we ask God not only to bless earthly resources, but also to "save us from our selfish use of what thou givest." We don't pray for God to save others from our selfishness, but to save *us* from our selfishness. Each time we acquire something at the cost of another's chance to thrive or even survive, we are ourselves diminished. Of course our selfishness means less for someone else, but the prayer reminds us that sacrifice for the well-being others also enriches and deepens our own lives

The disciple's task is to remember continually the interconnectedness of all persons, to see that the welfare of one directly affects the welfare of another. Every person who remembers that lives in a way that honors God and brings Jesus Christ to life on earth.

God's kingdom truly will have come when every human being can be nourished—physically, spiritually, and emotionally—without harming anyone else. Knowing that all persons make up the body of Christ, we must work to see that no one gets hurt in our efforts to prosper. Nothing will have to die to nourish us. Only then will we all live in the land of milk and honey.

Lord, grant us grace to live so that our fullness does not require another's emptiness.

Tuesday, Fifth Week of Lent

Our duty is to believe and trust in God;
to love and obey God and to bring others to know him;
to put nothing in the place of God;
to show God respect in thought, word, and deed;
and to set aside regular times for worship, prayer,
and the study of God's ways.

— The Catechism, p. 847

When a government—local, state, or national—faces a budget crisis, it often chooses to cut spending on infrastructure. Urgent needs can make building and maintenance on roads, bridges, and other basic systems and structures seem unimportant. Ultimately, though, nothing survives without a safe and efficient infrastructure.

The life of a Christian disciple follows the same pattern. We live in a world filled with need, with urgent demands for helping other people. If we're not careful, we can begin to think that there is so much work to do that we cannot afford the luxury of time for prayer, study, and worship.

Like government revenues, time runs in short supply for human beings, but prayer, worship, and study are not luxuries. They are the "infrastructure" that support our way to God. If we stop investing time in them, at some point our spiritual growth will cease and our spirits wither.

The Catechism asks the question, "What is our duty to God?" The answer includes believing in God, bringing others to know God, putting God at the center of our lives, and showing God respect "in thought, word, and deed." Believing, evangelizing, and centering our lives on God are important goals of our spiritual lives, but we cannot travel toward those goals without regular maintenance on the foundation that supports them.

The disciplines of worship, study of Scripture and devotional materials, and prayer are not luxuries to explore only when we have extra time. They form the essential infrastructure that allows us to travel the way of God.

We won't get far on that road if the bridges and roads are out.

God, grant us wisdom to maintain the groundwork of our spirituality.

Wednesday, Fifth Week of Lent

Hear the commandments of God to his people.

— The Decalogue, p. 350

Vacationing on the coast of Maine, I walked along the beach each day. I had to walk a good bit to reach the stairs that led safely down to water level. One day, I tried a shortcut, using a set of steps that had been blocked off. As soon as I put my foot on the first one, I knew why they were blocked. Rounded with wear, they were slick and dangerous.

Human nature often urges us to resist boundaries, to push back against restrictions, asserting our freedom and self-reliance. We rarely welcome rules, even something as basic as the Ten Commandments, because we see them as restrictive and cumbersome.

But like the dangerous steps I encountered, the actions forbidden in God's commandments are not arbitrarily chosen. God urges us to avoid those behaviors to protect us. God knows—and tries continually to remind us—that we can find inner peace and outward compassion only when we "follow the rules" of loving God and neighbor.

Often during the Lenten season, we say the Decalogue, or Ten Commandments, prefaced with these words, "Hear the commandments of God to his people." We then recite the familiar words which urge us to put God first and honor other human beings. Many bristle, though, at even these basic commandments, feeling that such rules encroach upon our precious free will.

Like any effective authority figure, God does not set forth rules capriciously. God gives us steps to follow that will lead us safely to abundant life and boundaries to keep us from behavior that we will regret. In other words, God doesn't give us commandments simply to make us feel the power of divine authority. God tries to keep us from taking steps that could harm us irrevocably.

Merciful Lord, remove our arrogance
and allow us to find safety in your commandments.

Thursday, Fifth Week of Lent

Our Father, who art in heaven,
hallowed be thy Name,
thy kingdom come, thy will be done,
on earth as it is in heaven.

— The Lord's Prayer, p. 364

A story I once read about another country's election of a reform candidate lamented that major change requires money. "Who," it asked, "will pay for the revolution?"

Meaningful change seldom comes easily. We almost certainly will not be asked to die for Jesus, but we will be asked to let parts of ourselves die so that God may live fully in us. To be transformed into disciples of Jesus Christ, we will have to sacrifice.

Many Christians pray the Lord's Prayer, but do we honestly think about what we're saying? Do we truly desire that "thy will be done, on earth as it is in heaven"? For to manifest God's will in this world will require us to let go of countless pets—habits, prejudices, viewpoints, perhaps even relationships—that are not godly or productive. Bringing heaven to earth means purifying ourselves of judgmentalism, pettiness, rationalization, and the exclusion of others.

Most of us have good intentions about following Christ's way. We don't think of ourselves as hypocritical or duplicitous, but our actions can demonstrate those traits. We speak of loving others, but don't hesitate to bash people from other political parties, cultures, religions, or races. We talk about forgiveness, but we won't allow God to forgive us for the sins we think are beyond divine mercy. We speak of Jesus, but then use Jesus' name as a blunt instrument against people who don't agree with us.

These sacrifices are the costs to be borne to transform first our own lives and then the rest of the world. Are we willing to take on such costs to bring the kingdom of God fully into the world we inhabit? What are we willing to give up to make it happen? Who will pay for the revolution?

God of power and might, teach us to understand and welcome the costs of change.

Friday, Fifth Week of Lent

Almighty and eternal God,
so draw our hearts to thee,
so guide our minds,
so fill our imaginations, so control our wills,
that we may be wholly thine…
and then use us, we pray thee, as thou wilt,
and always to thy glory and the welfare of thy people.

— A Prayer of Self-Dedication, p. 832

One shift in the current housing market has resulted in "McMansions"—huge, single-family homes—losing their appeal to homebuyers. Many are now being repurposed as group homes, suburban greenhouses, and for other uses. In the Prayer of Self-Dedication, we ask God to "so draw our hearts to thee, so guide our minds, so fill our imaginations, so control our wills, that we may be wholly thine." In a spiritual sense, we are asking God to give us bigger places in which to live, places expanded and then filled by God's presence.

But when God invites us to be broadened by the presence of the Holy Spirit, the new space does not necessarily make us more comfortable. The Prayer of Self-Dedication reminds us that we are to invite others in, to forgive as God forgives, to love as God loves. We pray not only for a larger heart, but also for the wisdom to allow God to "use us…always to thy glory and the welfare of thy people."

Our awareness of God's eternity—a reality that transcends the troubles of this world—allows us to live in greater comfort. But plenty of other people in our lives—those who hurt and those who seek to hurt others—also need a bigger space, a place to feel the grace of God at work. God expands our hearts to make room for those who cannot build such places themselves. What's the point of a huge dwelling place if we're not going to allow others into those wide-open spaces?

Heavenly Father, expand our hearts
and give us the courage to invite others in.

Saturday, Fifth Week of Lent

*For to your faithful people,
O Lord, life is changed, not ended.*

— Preface for Commemoration of the Dead, p. 382

Years ago in school, I studied Abraham Maslow's hierarchy of needs. Using a triangle to depict his theory, Maslow put self-actualization, the place where a person becomes "more and more what one is," at its top. In the spiritual life, though, we can be dragged down by attributes identified with the self. We see centeredness as a plus, but self-centeredness as a minus. We seek righteousness, but fight against self-righteousness. Serving is virtuous, but self-serving is not.

We may hesitate to become disciples of Christ because we fear the loss of our individuality. We worry that following Christ turns us into sheep, each looking and acting like the rest of the herd. In fact, nothing could be further from the truth. When we give up the negative aspects of self, like self-righteousness and self-centeredness, we peel away the patina developed to please the rest of the world. We find our true self, buried for years or even decades by our need for others' approval.

In our liturgy for the Commemoration of the Dead, we speak of eternal life in Christ, a life given us as followers of Jesus. In the process of being buried with Christ in baptism, the true self—the one God created us to be—is resurrected. Plunging into the waters of baptism and following Christ fully cleanses us of our need to posture for others. For when we share in Jesus' death, we also share in his Resurrection. We can only find our self by first shedding the baggage we carry around to meet others' expectations.

Self-centeredness dies in the waters of baptism, but a new center in the true self—the person God created each of us to be—emerges from those cleansing waters. And in that death leading to true life, the self is changed, not ended.

Risen Lord, bring the true self to light in each of us.

Palm Sunday

*Mercifully grant that we may walk
in the way of his suffering,
and also share in his Resurrection.*

— Liturgy for Palm Sunday, p. 272

In doctors' waiting rooms, people pass the time by reading ancient magazines, playing with cell phones, or simply fidgeting. Their restlessness always makes me wonder how a person waiting for a doctor can be called a patient. But the word comes from the Latin root word "pati" that speaks of suffering and enduring. People generally come to a doctor because they are suffering, trying to endure some form of pain or discomfort. The word passion comes from "passus," a verb form of the same root word. So when we say that someone has a passion for something, we may mean that they care enough to suffer for it.

Palm Sunday, the day we reenact Jesus' trial and execution, is often called the Sunday of the Passion. Back when I thought the word dealt only with romantic love, I could not understand using passion to describe Jesus' suffering and death. But on the Sunday of the Passion, we retell the story of Jesus' arrest, torture, and crucifixion. On this day we see how deeply God loves us. Remembering that "passion" comes from the root word for "suffering," we see in detail what God was willing to do to save us. As disciples, we ask in the Palm Sunday liturgy "that we may walk in the way of his suffering, and also share in his Resurrection."

Few followers of Christ today will be asked to endure physical torture and death for God. But are we willing to endure other human trials—embarrassment at not fitting in, acknowledgement of weakness, vulnerability, and need of forgiveness—for the love of God? Do we love God with a passion?

Lord God, allow us to love others
with the same passion you show for us.

Monday in Holy Week

*My soul doth magnify the Lord,
and my spirit hath rejoiced in God my Savior.*

— The Song of Mary, p. 50

Like most kids, I used to love playing with a magnifying glass. Though respectful of fire, I did enjoy using a magnifier to focus sunlight on paper long enough to burn a hole in it. I'm amazed that sunlight, around us all day long, can start a fire when carefully focused and yet does not imperil us.

Today is the day we remember the conception of Jesus. What would happen in our lives as disciples if we became like Mary, so obedient and so purely loving, that we could "magnify" the fire of the Lord? Like Mary, many of us will face significant trials as we prepare to bear the presence of God to others in the world. And we may have to endure much before the light of God within us becomes focused enough to burst into flame.

I love the words in the Magnificat: "My soul doth magnify the Lord, and my spirit hath rejoiced in God my Savior." But between the time she uttered those words and the time of Jesus' birth, Mary's waiting could not have been easy. She endured not only the typical physical challenges of pregnancy, but also a time of halting explanations, of questioning what she had heard, of wondering what would happen once this son came into the world.

Generally we say the Magnificat in Advent, another time focused on waiting. But during Holy Week we can also practice waiting. We can practice saying to God, if even for a short time, that we will obey with the pure heart of Mary. And if we continue to practice, perhaps our souls, too, can magnify the Lord.

God, give us obedient hearts and souls.

Tuesday in Holy Week

O God of grace and glory,
Give us faith to see in death the gate of eternal life,
so that in quiet confidence
we may continue our course on earth.

— The Burial of the Dead: Rite Two, p. 493

Scientists continue to study the case in which a man's brain changed dramatically after he had been beaten. After recovering from the attack, the man had remarkable mathematical ability. Apparently dormant sections of his brain were activated by the trauma.

The inactive, unknown parts of our souls can also be activated by trauma. Taught to be self-reliant and independent, we human beings begin to think we can control everything. Only with the introduction of a significant trauma—the loss of a loved one, a job, or some other precious dimension of life—do we begin to see our need for God. Trauma can bring gifts to life that we never knew existed.

Every disciple's faith in Jesus' Resurrection is tested at times of loss. Yet in the Burial Office, we celebrate our belief in resurrection. In the prayers of that liturgy, we ask God to "Give us faith to see in death the gate of eternal life, so that in quiet confidence we may continue our course on earth."

Perhaps we should pray that prayer not only at the physical death of a person, but in the smaller, emotional deaths we suffer when circumstances do not meet our hopes or expectations. We draw closer to God if we can learn to see each of those deaths as a "gate of eternal life" that can help us "continue our course on earth."

No one would choose to endure devastating losses; we don't even want the little deaths that each day brings. But it may be that only in such traumas are the deepest, God-seeking portions of our souls are activated.

Dear God, use the small deaths we die each day
to form us in your image.

Wednesday in Holy Week

We thank you, Almighty God, for the gift of water.

— Holy Baptism, Thanksgiving over the Water, p. 306

In times of severe drought, the observation is often made that it can teach us to use water resources more wisely. No one wishes for drought, but a lack of water can help us appreciate its importance.

This week, as we remember the last days of Jesus' earthly life, we can consider a different kind of drought—spiritual drought. We can try to imagine the last days of Jesus' earthly life through the eyes of those who did not yet know there would be a resurrection. This exercise can guard against complacency about our salvation—and even the most faithful disciple can sometimes forget how impossible life would be without Jesus Christ.

Once we imagine life without God, we will be moved more often to give thanks for the gift of God's salvation. It is the same gratitude we offer at each baptismal service when we pray, "We thank you, Almighty God, for the gift of water." In that prayer, we not only prepare to welcome others into the body of Christ, but we remember our own gratitude for the grace of God's salvation.

The experiences of Holy Week give us the opportunity to practice that gratitude. Each day of our Christian lives, we live into the gift of baptism, a gift that offers abundant life every moment of our human lives. It is appropriate that we thank God for the waters of baptism at each baptismal service. And we are even more grateful for those waters when we remember that many others live in drought.

Almighty God, remind us daily of the gifts given to us in the waters of baptism.

Maundy Thursday

By this shall the world know that you are my disciples: That you have love for one another.

— Liturgy for Maundy Thursday, p. 275

I once joined a softball team after the season had begun, and for my first game, I had to find my new team among many others at a sports complex. To save me time and energy, a team member had told me, "When you get to the fields, we'll probably be the only ones wearing purple shirts."

I sometimes wish it could be that easy to tell good people from evil. If we all wore uniforms or bore some other outward indication of our inward grace (or lack thereof), we could save a great deal of time sorting "us" from "them." But given the fickle nature of the human heart, no one fits consistently into one category. Good, virtuous people can make horrible choices, and people we have written off as ungodly can still accomplish God's work.

As our liturgy for Maundy Thursday concludes, we hear these words, "By this shall the world know that you are my disciples: That you have love for one another." In the humble and selfless act of serving his disciples, Jesus shows us that we need no uniforms because there are no teams. When he says that his disciples "have love for one another," he implicitly tells us to stop making distinctions between us and them. He warns against judging others, because it separates us one from another and slows the coming of God's kingdom to earth.

As we enter the last days of this Lenten season, we remember Jesus' stunning choice to serve us, even though he is the Son of God. We are Christians and his disciples. We may differ from one another in countless ways, but a passerby should be able to spot us by the single uniform we all wear—"That we have love for one another."

Gentle Lord, train us to
love one another as you love us.

Good Friday

O God, make speed to save us.
O Lord, make haste to help us.

— Compline, p. 128

I once worked with a woman who got on my nerves. Like many who follow the way of Christ yet fall into pettiness, I began to think of her as my "cross to bear."

By that phrase, we usually mean that we have no other choice and must resign ourselves to the burden placed on us. But when we describe a person or circumstance as our "cross to bear," we miss entirely the concept of Christ's bearing of the cross. Jesus was not forced to endure the cross. Reconciled with the Father's will, he took it up willingly.

As disciples, we, too, take up our crosses willingly, though admitting that we cannot bear such weight with our own strength. And so, we pray on Good Friday and every day that brings unthinkable burdens, "O God, make speed to save us; O Lord, make haste to help us."

When walking the Stations of the Cross, I often wonder what Simon of Cyrene did after he helped carry Jesus' cross. Scripture says that he was compelled to take up the cross. But afterward, did he, with pride, tell his friends about his involvement? Did he hide his participation? Did he wish he could have done more to help the tortured and exhausted Jesus?

God does not intend for the disciples of Christ to bear the weight of the world. God asks us to live with commitment and joy, taking up burdens willingly. We can do that, because we know we will never bear the weight of the cross alone. We take it up and do what we can do. And then, when we can no longer stand or move forward, we pray, "O God, make speed to save us; O Lord, make haste to help us."

Lord, give us the courage to accept burdens willingly in your name.

Holy Saturday

O God of unchangeable power and eternal light:
Look favorably on your whole Church…
let the whole world see and know that things
which were cast down are being raised up,
and things which had grown old are being made new.

— Liturgy for the Easter Vigil, p. 291

In a science course I took years ago, the teacher asked us how boats can stay afloat when their raw materials would sink quickly. The question fascinated me then, and I still don't understand the answer.

I also cannot understand how the eternal stays afloat in the human world. Human sin, error, and selfishness weigh too heavily for the grace of God to live in us. Yet despite the weight of those raw materials, we find God in human life. We see the eternal at work here, in the ponderous temporal.

In the Easter Vigil, we ask God to "Look favorably on your whole Church" and "let the whole world see and know that things which were cast down are being raised up, and things which had grown old are being made new." In mentioning "your whole Church," the prayers embrace the flaws of that human institution, offering hope that God's eternal purposes will be accomplished despite its imperfections.

People who do not embrace the Christian faith may have been burned by experiences in the institutional Church that have convinced them that the eternal matters of God cannot live in human institutions and hearts. They also often believe that our faith offers only an afterlife. Both opinions stem from equating the concept of the eternal with endless time. But instead, eternal refers to something in this life that transcends time entirely.

As disciples of Christ, we can begin to teach others to see the eternal in the present moment. To one who does not know the God of Jesus Christ, the idea of experiencing the eternal in this present life must look like a contradiction. After all, how can the heaviness of human life float in the waters of eternity?

God, lift us to your presence
despite the weight of our imperfection.

Easter Day

The Lord Almighty grant us a peaceful night and a perfect end.

— Compline, p. 127

As a child, I once told an older, meaner child the error of his ways. But knowing his brute strength meant he could do whatever he wanted, he replied, "What are you going to do about it?"

If we consider the daunting ways of this world, we may feel that same sense of helplessness I felt at that moment. We can see more clearly now, after our Lenten training, prayer, and reflection, how very much goes wrong in our world. We see the hunger—both physical and spiritual—in our own backyards. We see how often brutality wins out, how often the rich get richer at the expense of the poor. And our temptation may be to raise our palms to the sky, in helpless frustration, convinced that we can do nothing to change such systems.

But now we have reached the day of the church year when we particularly remember the Resurrection of our Lord Jesus Christ. More than any other time, we celebrate the victory of Jesus Christ over death, our most feared enemy. We celebrate the knowledge that even death cannot conquer those who live and die with Christ.

Shouldn't the knowledge that nothing in this world can hurt us empower us to challenge all oppression of the human spirit? Shouldn't our new freedom in Christ, highlighted this Easter Sunday, give us courage to believe that the world can and should be better than it is? Shouldn't our knowledge of the risen Christ make us bold enough to challenge the status quo, even where we benefit from the current system?

With Christ's triumph over the tomb, the Lord has granted us "a peaceful night." But the "perfect end" can only come when we push back against oppressive and unjust systems. The Lord is risen indeed. And yet, the world still is not what it should be. As disciples of Christ, what are we going to do about it?

Gentle God, strengthen us to live out in our actions the faith we proclaim in words.

The Rev. Carol Mead is the Episcopal chaplain at Mississippi State University and the assisting priest at the Episcopal Church of the Resurrection in Starkville, Mississippi. She writes meditations on the Daily Office each weekday for www.holyordinary.com.